Carving

Classic Female Figures

in Wood

by Ian Norbury

Fox
Chapel Publishing

1970 Broad Street • East Petersburg, PA 17520
www.FoxChapelPublishing.com

Carving Classic Female Figures in Wood is an original work, first published in 2004 by Fox Chapel Publishing Company, Inc. The patterns contained herein are copyrighted by the author. Artists who purchase this book may make up to three photocopies of each pattern for personal use. Publication of patterns and any other portion of this book for resale or distribution under any other circumstances is a violation of copyright law.

Publisher	Alan Giagnocavo
Editor	Ayleen Stellhorn
Editorial Assistant	Gretchen Bacon
Cover Design	Jon Deck
Layout	Linda Eberly, Eberly Designs

ISBN 1-56523-221-6

Library of Congress Control Number: 2004102181

To order your copy of this book,
please send check or money order
for the cover price plus $3.50 shipping to:
Fox Chapel Publishing
Book Orders
1970 Broad St.
East Petersburg, PA 17520

Or visit us on the Web at **www.FoxChapelPublishing.com**

Printed in China
10 9 8 7 6 5 4 3 2 1

DEDICATION

This book is dedicated to four beautiful girls: my grandchildren Katherine, Jennifer, Julia and Chloe.

ACKNOWLEDGMENTS

I would like to thank photographer Keith Cooper and model Donna for providing the excellent photographs; also, Sharon Valenzuela for translating my appalling handwriting into type.

TO OUR READERS

This book includes photographs of professional models in the nude as reference material for the projects in this book. The publisher and the author believe that these images are necessary for the artist to understand and render the female form.

TABLE OF CONTENTS

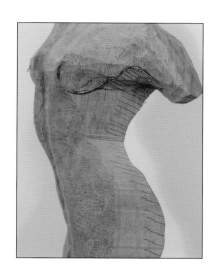
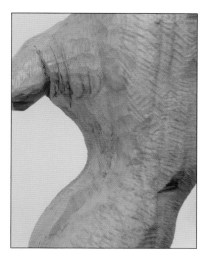

Chapter Three

Carving a Walnut Torso . . 47

ABOUT THE AUTHOR

Ian Norbury was born in Sheffield, England, in 1948 and was educated in Hampshire. After selling his first picture at the age of 15 and being dismissed from the woodworking class, he began his career as an artist, selling pictures from local galleries until he went to Cyprus in 1965. He worked in Cyprus for six years painting portraits and landscapes and decorating nightclubs until 1971 when he returned to the United Kingdom to marry Betty. He continued painting, mainly racehorses, until 1975 when he went to St. Paul's College, Cheltenham, to study art education. Here he continued to develop his growing interest in three-dimensional art, particularly woodcarving. When he graduated in 1980, he set up a woodcarving studio in an old bakery near the center of Cheltenham.

Ian rose rapidly through the ranks of British woodcarvers, having a solo exhibition every year, regularly contributing to magazines, and writing his first book, *Techniques of Creative Woodcarving*, in 1983. This book is still in print in three languages and is sold worldwide.

Several more books followed as well as seminars and workshops in Switzerland, Iceland, Australia, New Zealand, Ireland, Canada and America. Ian's two three-month tours of the United States have covered many major cities, and his ability as a teacher has created a huge demand for his services. He was the first woodcarver to produce teaching CDs. These are in his own inimitable style, and as one student put it, "…it is like standing at the great man's shoulder while he works."

Ian's ability as a wood sculptor is based on his skilled draftsmanship and a pragmatic technical approach, which get the job done as efficiently as possible regardless of method. His innovative techniques are matched by his original and imaginative subjects, which have given him financial success and an enviable reputation among art lovers in Britain.

Much of his work is based on European folklore and mythology, combined with cynical tongue-in-cheek sideswipes at the pomposity of contemporary life. This perspective finds an easy rapport with audiences. His great technical expertise in the rendering of detail and his acute observations of expressions and appearances are irresistible to many people. In recent years his innovative use of mixed timbers, inlays of colored woods, metals, stones, shells and gems has given his work new impetus. Of course he is equally known for his exquisitely made nude figures and portrait busts, which are the usual subjects of his teaching seminars.

Ian now lives with his wife, Betty, in the Republic of Ireland, but still maintains a house, studio and gallery in England.

INTRODUCTION

For thousands of years the depiction of the female body has been a constant obsession with artists and craftsmen, from the crudest daub on a cave wall through the finest marble sculptures, bronzes and paintings to the mystifying productions of cubism and abstraction. For most artists it seems to be a field that, once they get into it, they cannot leave it alone. I have had the same experience myself. I keep plugging away at nudes, not really knowing what I am trying to achieve, but knowing that I have not achieved it yet.

I hope that you will have the same experience and get the same challenge from carving nudes that I have. And get this idea in your head right from the start: You are trying to carve a nude the way you want it; you are not trying to make a reproduction of a real woman out of a block of wood 12 inches high. That would be as absurd as it sounds. Go to your local bookstore or library. Look through a few art history books and see for yourself the bizarre and endless array of interpretations of the female form. In this book I am providing only a starting point.

Bacchante

Bacchantes were the female followers of Bacchus, the Roman god of wine. When intoxicated on wine infused with ivy leaves, groups of Bacchantes would seek out men and tear them to pieces.
30" high

The Four Seasons
Left to right: Spring, Summer, Autumn (Fall) and Winter.
In these carvings, I have translated the traditional theme of the
cycle of the seasons into womanhood. Spring is a young girl, shy
and not fully developed. Summer is fully mature, vigorous and
aware of her own body. Autumn is placid, ripe and content,
while Winter is sadder and beginning to fade. Each torso was
carved from pitch pine in 1986 and is somewhat stylized.
Each figure: 18" x 5" x 5" including plinth

Walnut Torso
This exuberant figure is carved from a large
block of beautiful walnut.
30" high

Bronze Torso
This bronze started out as a woodcarving that I then copied in plaster and had cast in bronze. This figure is my only excursion into that medium, which I found a very tedious and disappointing process.

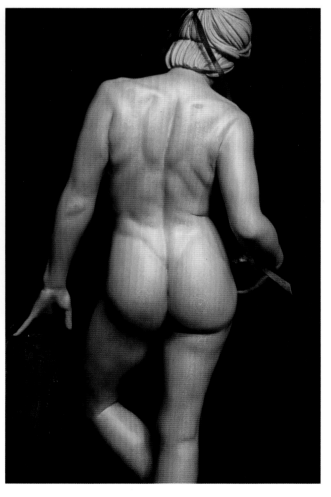

Detail of Atalanta
This figure shows the effect of copying a live model exactly as seen, resulting in a rather homely looking woman, but not really what one expects in a sculptured nude.
15" high

Stone Torsos
I carved this pair of torsos in Malta from the soft, local limestone, large blocks of which can be purchased for less than five dollars. Soft stone is far easier to carve than wood and is worth a try.
24" high

TAKING PHOTOGRAPHS & CREATING PATTERNS

The lady in the photographs is a professional model who has tried her best to adopt an identical pose for eight separate pictures. This is virtually impossible and inevitably there will be variations in the different views.

Bear in mind always that a nude, unless it is a portrait of an individual, is not a reproduction of a person with his or her clothes off. A nude is the creation of the artist. The model is a guide, not a blueprint.

Taking photographs

Taking photographs of a live model for carving is quite difficult. If the camera is at waist height, it is looking up at the model's head and down at her feet.

Look carefully at **Figure 1**. Here you will see that the right elbow is level with the

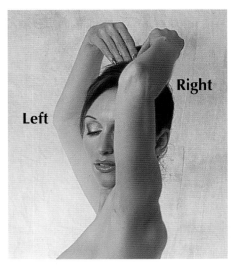

Figure 1

Figure 2

In comparing these two photographs, you will notice that the positions of the elbows are reversed. In Figure 1 the right elbow is level with the forehead and the left elbow is level with the top of the head. In Figure 2 the right elbow is level with the top of the head and the left elbow is level with the forehead.

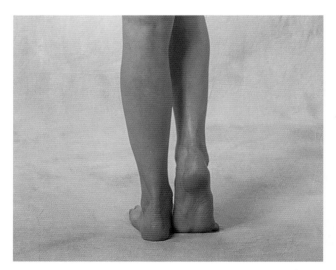

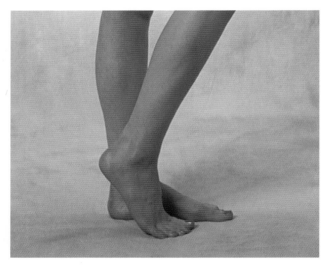

Figure 3

Figure 4

Camera angles and lenses can affect how an image appears on film. In Figure 3 it is clear that the model is standing on a level floor. In Figure 4 the model is still standing on the same level floor, but her feet appear to be on different planes.

forehead and the left elbow is level with the top of the head. Now look at **Figure 2**. You will see that the right elbow is level with the top of the head and the left elbow is level with the forehead. The positions are reversed.

Now study **Figure 3** and **Figure 4**. In Figure 3 it is clear that the model is standing on a flat, horizontal surface. In Figure 4 the far foot appears higher than the nearer one, even though the model is still standing on the same flat, horizontal surface.

All of this is very obvious, but clearly the pictures cannot be used as they are for the basis of working drawings. Some redrawing is necessary.

These effects, which are worse on some camera lenses than others, can be reduced by using a longer lens and moving farther and farther away from the model. Thus, from a distance of 30 feet the pictures would be far more accurate. An even better method than this one is to take a series of photographs at floor, hip, shoulder and

eye levels. From eight positions—front, back, both sides and the four points between—this makes a total of 32 photographs. The front, back and side views are obviously most important. The point: If you have a model and a camera you are very lucky, so make the most of it.

Making plans

The problems set out above are not so great on a torso because the extremes of the figure are not being used, but some judgment is still required to make accurate plans.

Clearly, the front view gives a fairly accurate representation of the dynamics of the figure; therefore, this pose is used as the basic position.

To begin making plans, first make a photocopied enlargement of the front view. Then by very accurate measurement of the height of the figure in the front and side photographs, enlarge the side view to exactly the same size as the front view. **(See Figure 5.)** Trace the outlines of the model.

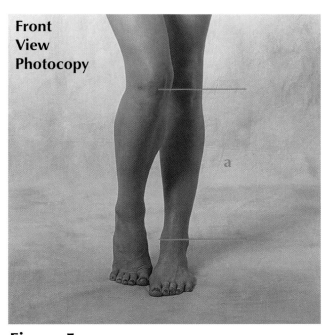

Front View Photocopy

a

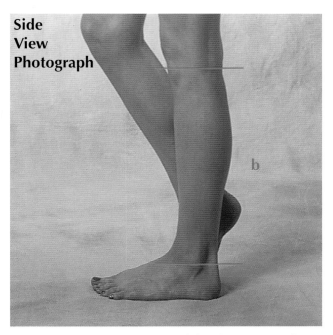

Side View Photograph

b

Figure 5: Photocopy and enlarge the front view to the desired size. Measure the height of the photocopy and use the formula below to figure out how much to enlarge or reduce the side view.

PHOTOCOPY HEIGHT (a)	÷	PHOTOGRAPH HEIGHT (b)	=	MULTIPLYING FACTOR TO ENLARGE/REDUCE PHOTOGRAPH (c)
41 mm	÷	54 mm	=	0.75%

Fix the two photocopies on a drawing board precisely level at a certain point—the bottom of the breast, for example. **(See Figure 6, Line A.)** Now, from significant points on the front view, rule horizontal lines across to the side view. **(See Figure 6, Lines B–I.)** This exercise will show you where the points on the side view should actually be and how to position the pictures accordingly.

Looking at the drawing, you can see that the lower edge of the right breast and an estimated line of the true floor surface are both level. However, the feet are clearly wrong and the left knee is too low on the front view. The arms are also very inaccurate on the side view.

In the revised details the arms, feet and knees have been redrawn to make both views coincide. **(See Figure 6, red illustrations.)**

Creating drawings

My next step is to create drawings from the patterns and the photographs. In these drawings I attempt to rationalize the surface forms of the figure into more clearly defined areas. **(See Figures 7, 8, 9 and 10.)** These illustrations are not anatomical drawings, but more indicators of what to look for in the photographs.

As you'll notice, some of the shapes are not discernable on the photographs of the model. It would take a book full of pictures using different light sources to bring out all the shapes on the body. These drawings help to define those

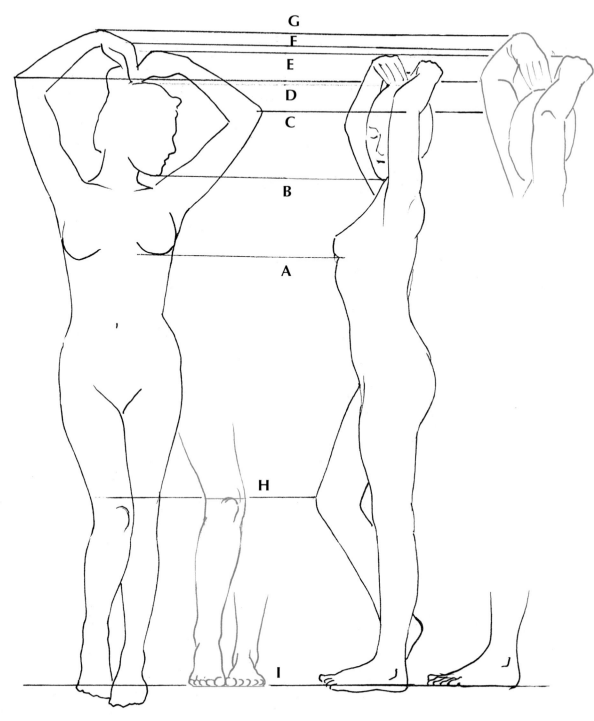

Figure 6

This figure shows outlines traced from the enlarged photocopies. Line A is used to align the two plans correctly. Notice that the feet, the left knee and the arms on the side view are not in alignment. The red illustrations show the corrections that need to be made to reconcile the two outlines.

shapes.

The final step is to create patterns based on the photographs, the plans and the drawings. You'll find the patterns for this model in the next chapter where I'll also show you how to carve this piece.

The anatomy diagrams

Knowledge of anatomy would be a wonderful asset for any figure carver. I have studied anatomy for twenty years, and it is still a problem. People vary so much—different body proportions, different muscular development, different fat deposits—all of which tends to make nonsense of anatomy diagrams. Most anatomy drawings seem to be uniformly based on male bodybuilders, showing sharply defined muscles where ordinary people have empty, sagging skin.

Furthermore, many of the surface muscles shown in the diagrams are only thin sheets that actually reveal the structures underneath.

However, a good book on anatomy—used as a diagrammatic basis from which to work, and which can then be adjusted to your own ideals—is probably the easiest way to work and is the method I use. I recommend *Human Anatomy for Artists* by Eliot Goldfinger as the most comprehensive book I have found to date.

Of course, the ideal solution when you do not understand a part of anatomy is to look at a real, live person. For the purposes of this book, I have included photographs of a live model at the beginning of each demonstration and anatomy sketches throughout the demonstrations as relevant to carving that particular part of the torso.

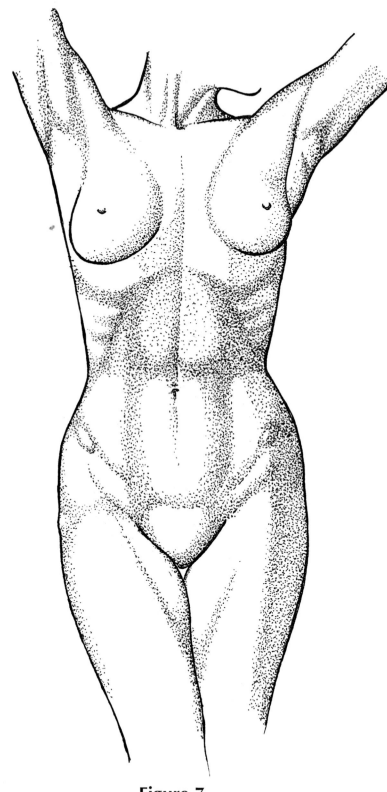

Figure 7

Shaded drawings of the outlines, based on the photographs and some anatomical knowledge, show more detail. These details are not always obvious on photographs due to lighting conditions and camera position.

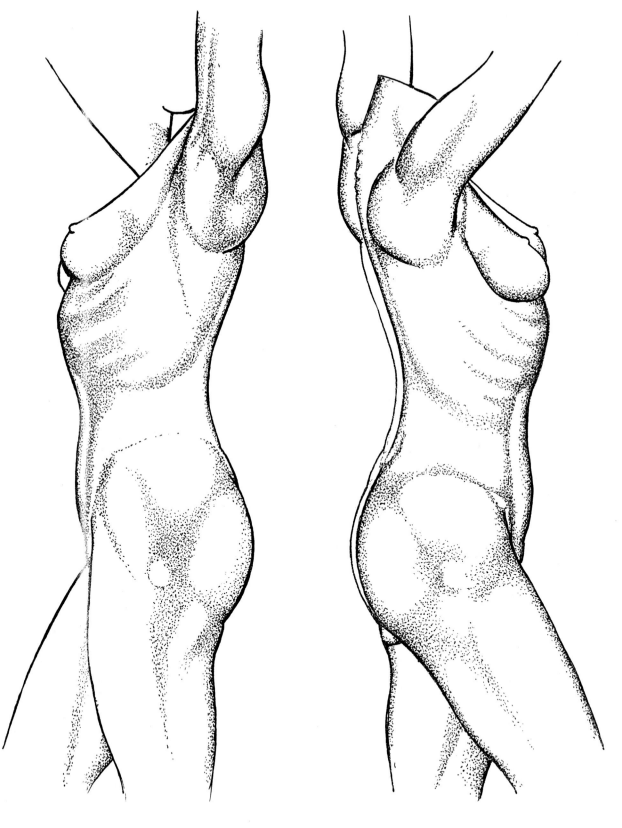

Figure 8

Figure 9

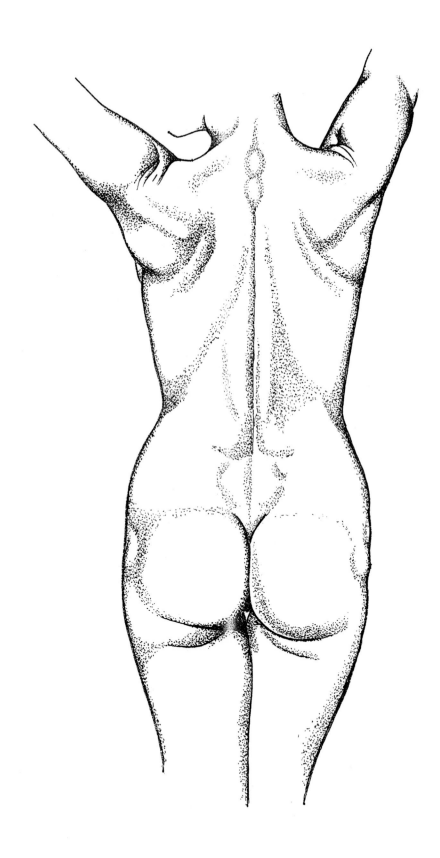

Figure 10

CARVING A LIMEWOOD TORSO

The actual removal of wood on a torso is very simple. Much of it can be carried out with a couple of gouges or even a rasp. It is not knowing which bits to cut off that creates the problems.

I have not included a tool list for this project because your choice of tools will change depending on the size of your carving. Any reasonable selection of gouges will be sufficient to complete the torso shown here.

By carefully carrying out this project, you will gain a greater understanding of the form of the torso and the underlying structures and, perhaps most importantly, acquire a systematic method of working from a concept through the various stages to a finished piece. This method can be applied to many more projects.

Limewood has many great advantages. In Europe, it is a very common tree, particularly in cities where it seems to thrive on concrete and smog. It grows to a great girth, has no discernable sapwood, mills easily, and dries quickly with little splitting. Because of its cell structure, it carves more easily than any other wood I know and will take the very finest, delicate detail. It sands to a fine finish and stains and polishes well. Basswood, if not the very same tree, is certainly a very close American cousin and is, for all intents and purposes of this book, identical.

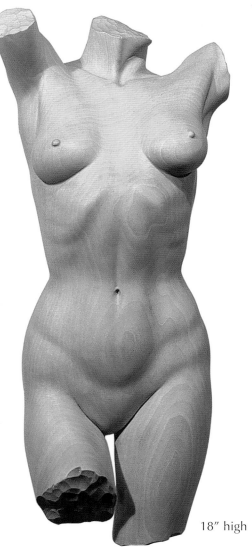

18″ high

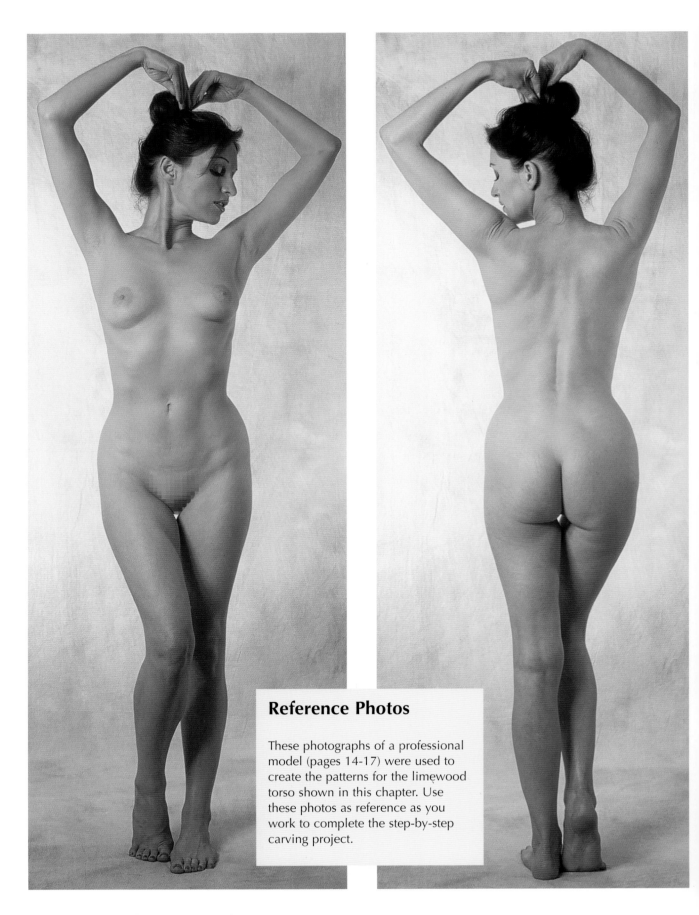

Reference Photos

These photographs of a professional model (pages 14-17) were used to create the patterns for the limewood torso shown in this chapter. Use these photos as reference as you work to complete the step-by-step carving project.

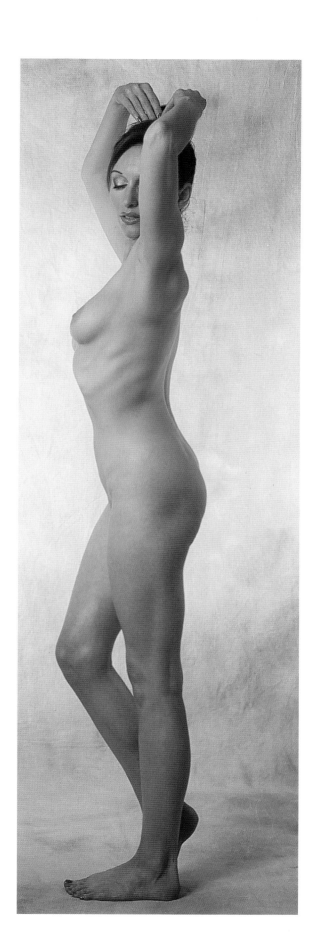

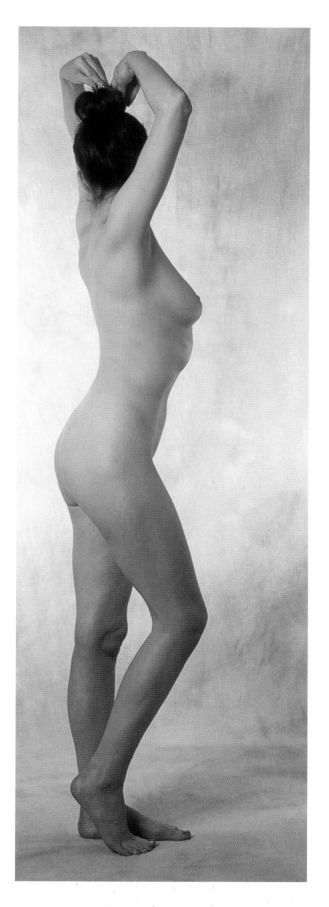

LIMEWOOD TORSO

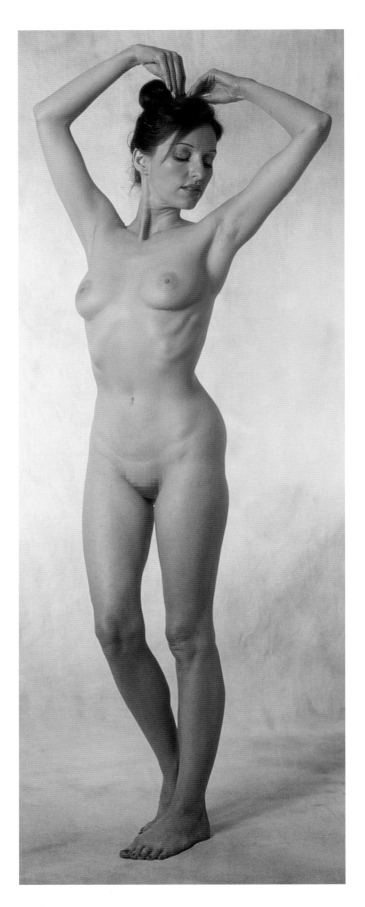

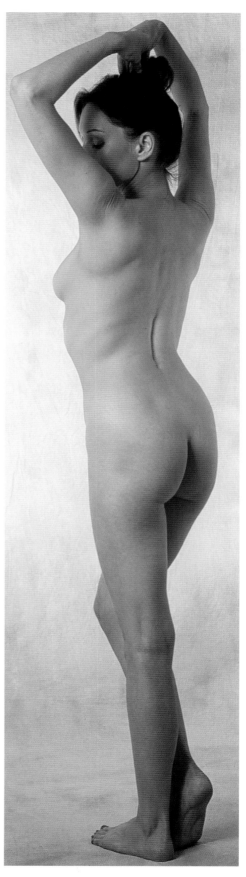

Limewood Torso
©Ian Norbury

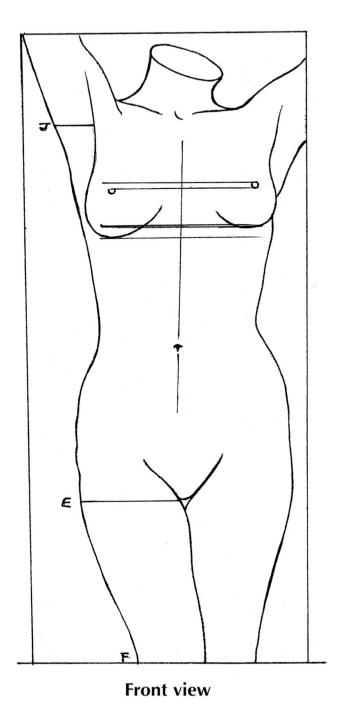

Front view

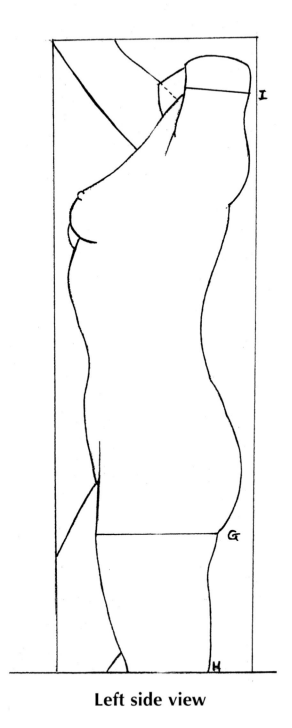

Left side view

Use the front and side views shown here to bandsaw the blank. Cut very carefully, precisely on the line. Remember that tracing the plans onto a block of wood and bandsawing them allows for considerable accumulative errors. Only by taking great care can you reduce these errors to a minimum.

Limewood Torso
©Ian Norbury

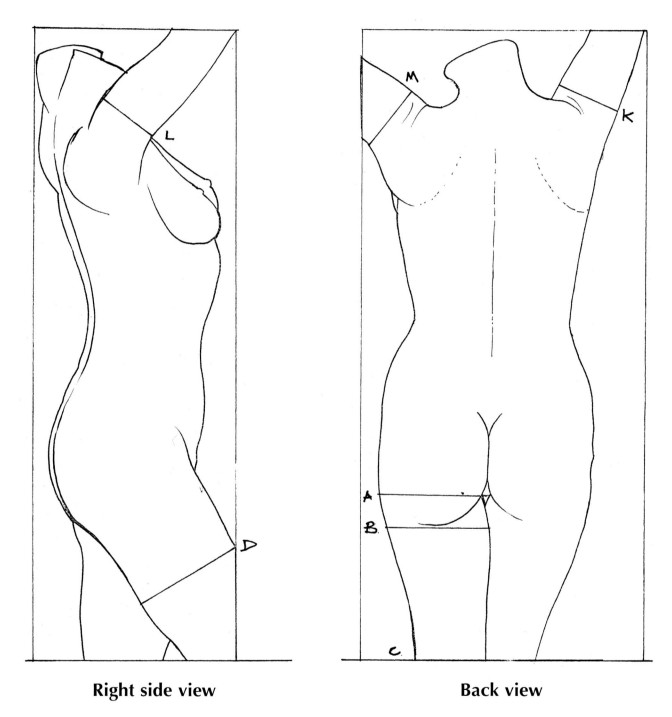

Right side view   **Back view**

The back and opposite side views are provided to show carving details.

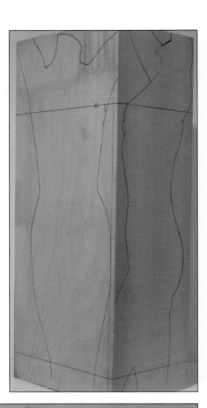

1 Enlarge the drawings to fit the size of wood you choose. My block is 19" x 5½" x 7½". The block must be planed perfectly square or the bandsawing will be inaccurate. Trace the front and the right-side drawings onto two adjacent sides of the block. Use the right nipple as a datum line to align the drawings. Only the outline is needed. Leave a piece at the base so the carving can be held in a vise or clamp.

2 Bandsaw the front view. Notice that the cut is as close to the line as possible, thereby ensuring that the dimensions of the sawn blank are identical to the drawings. Make sure the bandsaw blade is perfectly square to the table. Always follow the manufacturer's safety instructions.

Note: The words "left" and "right," when used throughout the demonstration that follows, always refer to left and right as seen on the figure from the front. Therefore, what appears to be the left side when looking at a photo of the back of the carving is still referred to as the right side.

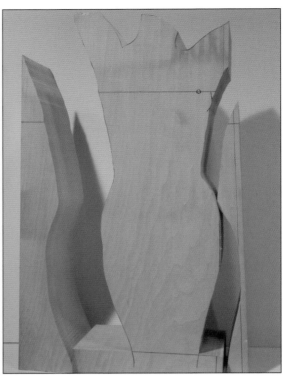

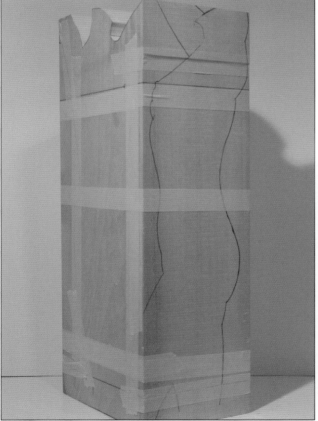

3 Use masking tape to securely fasten the two main pieces of waste in place. You are now ready to make the second cut. More tape will need to be added during the bandsawing process as areas are cut away.

4 The main areas of waste must now be marked on the wood. Mount the blank on a vise or clamp. Using a pair of dividers, measure the dimensions of the limbs. First measure the positions lines A – H on the patterns (pages 18 and 19). Mark the lines on your carving and then measure the width of the limb at those points. Measure and draw precisely, not approximately.

5 Mark the waste wood to be removed on the right leg. This area is in front of the leg that is pushed back. Also mark the waste wood to be removed behind the left shoulder.

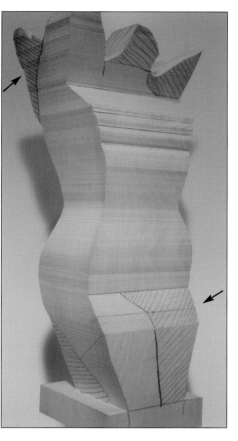

6 Mark the waste wood to be removed from the back of the left leg. This area is behind the leg that is pushed forward. Also mark the waste wood to be removed in front of the right shoulder.

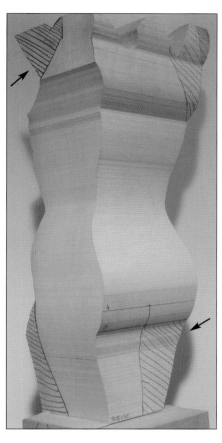

7 Start to remove the waste using a half round gouge, then flatten the surfaces with a flatter gouge. The waste in the corner of the legs at the back and at the front must be cut into a neat square corner. This ensures that the dimensions remain the same throughout the widths of the limbs.

8 The cuts that remove the waste wood at the back of the left shoulder must curve from the shoulder up to the line of the neck, then taper away to the line of the shoulder blade. (See Step 5.) The cuts at the front of the right shoulder (See Step 6.) and at the front right of the neck also have to curve up the neck (See Figure 26.). Check the sizes of the upper arms using lines I – L. M and K should be the same and I and L should be the same.

LIMEWOOD TORSO

9 The right breast is slightly higher than the left, because the left arm is angled forward, the right arm is pulling upward. Remove a small amount of waste below the right breast to raise it; remove a small amount above the left breast, to lower it. Mark the waste wood to be removed above the left breast. Remember to leave wood for the nipple, as shown.

10 Mark the waste wood to be removed below the right breast.

11 Next, mark the waste wood to be removed between the breasts.

12 Scoop out the area between the breasts down to the level of the breastbone, which runs in a straight line up the center of the chest.

13 Mark the waste wood to be removed from the front of the neck. This area forms the inside surface of the left arm across to the right shoulder and can be cut into a square corner in the throat.

14 This area has now been removed. The area around the neck is the most complicated part of this carving and is hard to visualize. Careful measurement and precise cutting are vital. Mark the dimensions of the neck and draw the circular shape on the top.

15 Now mark the waste wood to be removed from the back of the neck. This curved piece is the extension of bandsawing the shoulder.

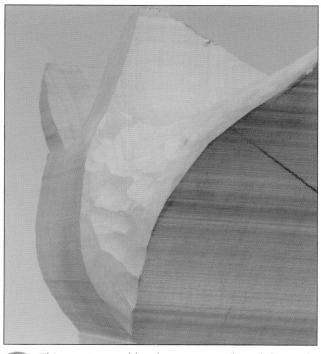

16 This waste wood has been removed, and the neck should now have its true dimensions.

17 You can now proceed to round off the figure. Starting on the right side, draw a line from the highest points, running down the muscles around the shoulder blade, down the ribcage to the hip and thigh (A). On the front of the body, draw a line down the leading edge of the ribcage and along the side of the stomach muscles (B). Draw another line from the front of the hipbone down the middle of the thigh (C). You will also need to draw the side view of the breast.

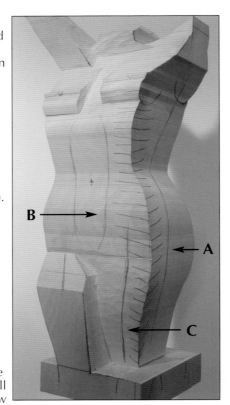

18 This corner from the bottom of the breast to the baseline of the figure can now be rounded off. Leave the centerlines untouched because they represent the profile the figure. You are basically trying to create a circular shape from a square one, so the waste wood you are removing should leave a quarter-circle. The completed cuts are seen here. Now repeat this step on the left side.

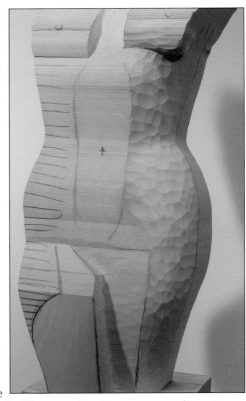

19 Draw a line down the center of the back of the left arm, running down the high point of the shoulder blade and down the column of muscle at the side of the spine, across the buttock and down the thigh (A). Draw another line down the outside of the left arm, along the rib cage, across the hip and down the thigh (B). Mark the wood between the lines for removal.

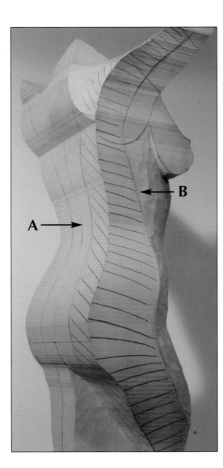

20 Round off this corner and repeat the procedure on the other side. The back of the carving should now look like this. Notice that the lines marking the high points are still intact.

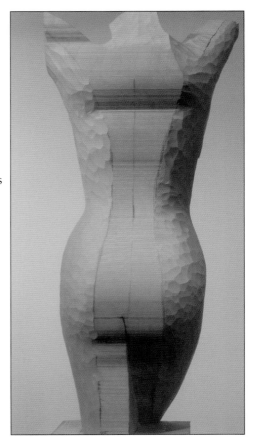

21 You now have to round off some minor areas at the front: the top inside of the left thigh, the two lower corners of the left arm, the top corner of the right arm and the front of the neck. Mark the waste wood in these areas for removal, as shown.

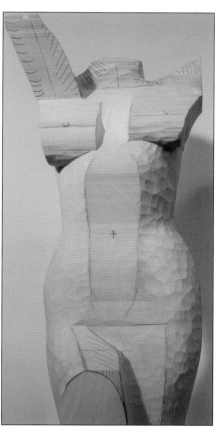

22 This stage is complete. Notice that the areas between the neck and the shoulders are scooped into curves rather than square corners.

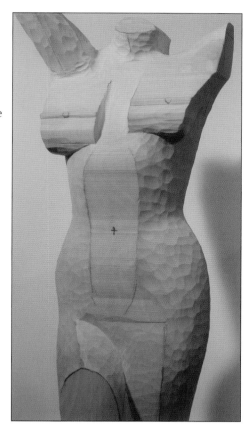

23 Returning to the back, mark the waste wood to be rounded off on the inside corners of both arms. This shaping runs into the shoulder and up the back corner of the neck. Also mark the inside corner of the right leg to be rounded.

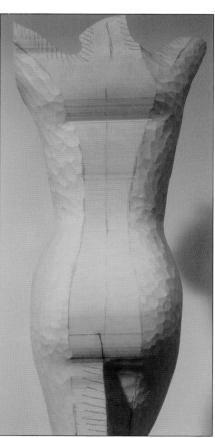

24 Remove the wood from these areas.

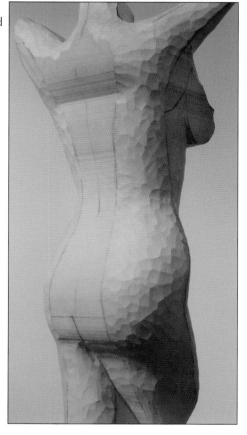

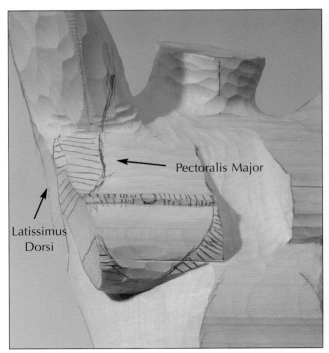

Pectoralis Major

Latissimus Dorsi

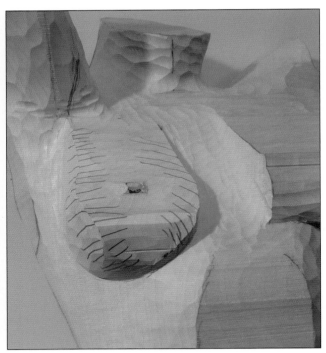

25 Measure the position of the left nipple and mark this on the carving. Then mark the lower inside and outside curves. Measure Line J (page 18) and mark in the line of the muscle from the upper arm to the breast. On the side, measure and mark the back line of the breast, running up to the armpit.

26 Cut the lower curves of the breast straight in to the level of the ribcage. The area at the side can be cut away, but leave a round gouge cut in the corner. The waste wood on both sides of the nipple is also removed. Finally, round over the two edges of the breast.

27 Mark the waste wood as shown and repeat this process on the right breast.

28 Notice that the breasts are mounted on the curve of the ribcage and point outward at an angle, not straight forward.

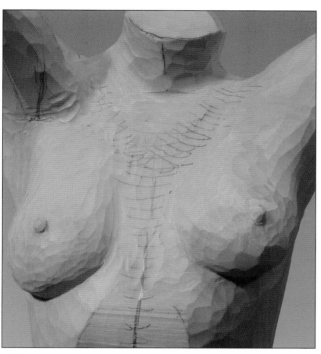

29 The breastbone, or sternum, forms a hollow down the chest, particularly near its lower end. This levels out toward the neck. The shoulder muscles, being raised, therefore, form the hollows between themselves and the neck. Together this forms a "Y" shape. Mark the wood to be removed.

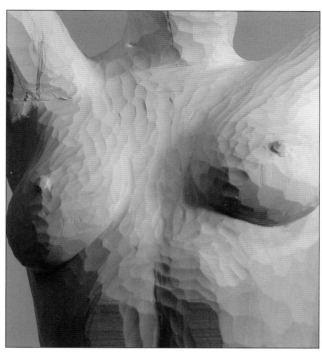

30 Remove the waste wood from the breastbone. This area is now complete.

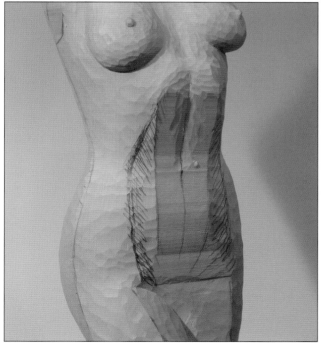

31 The stomach requires careful study. In the photograph on page 16, you can clearly see the ribcage curving outward and backward. In the center are the stretched stomach muscles. Below the ribs at the sides are two large muscles running down to the sides of the pelvis. Between these and the stomach muscles is a pronounced hollow. (See also Figure 8, page 11.)

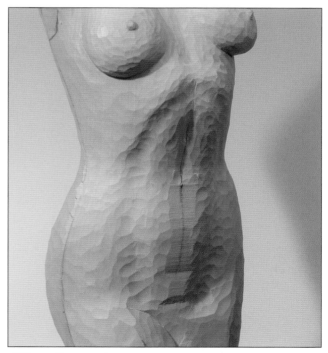

32 Following the markings, carve two large furrows running down the arch of the ribcage and down both sides of the stomach. Round off the stomach as it curves upward from these furrows. Leave the centerline and the navel as high points. Compare your progress with the photograph on page 16.

33 Moving to the bottom of the stomach and thighs, you can see in the photograph on page 16 that the thighs do not actually touch. The inside of the right thigh and the rear edge of the left thigh must be rounded to separate them. Mark the wood to be removed in these areas.

34 Clearly, if the left leg overlaps the right, the space between them must be at a slight angle.

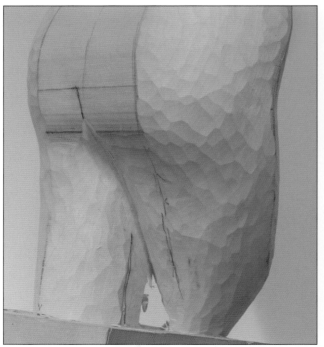

35 The thighs must be very carefully shaped, working from the back and the front to create the opening. If the cuts from the back and the front do not line up, a serious fault can be created.

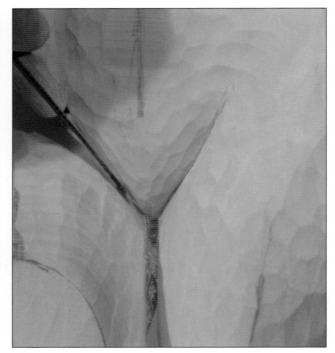

36 As cuts for the opening reach the top of the thighs, remove wood from the pubic bone. It curves backward between the legs and is rounded over on both sides. The deep fold between the fat pad on the pubic bone and the bulge at the top of the thigh is cut in with a knife.

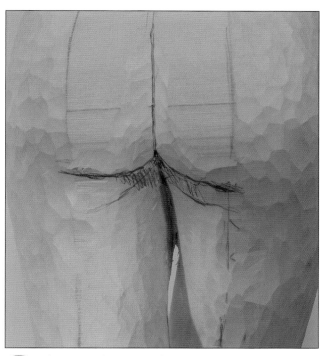

37 The triangular gap at the top of the thighs must be at the same height in the back and in the front. Measure this distance from the baseline and mark it on the centerline. Notice that the left buttock is slightly lower than the right because of the left leg's being thrust forward.

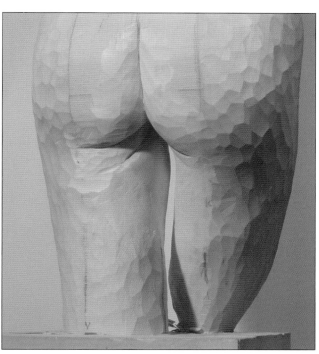

38 Completing the shaping of this area between the legs is very difficult. When the space is finally cut through, you may find it easier to shape and clean up with a strip of 80-grit sanding cloth.

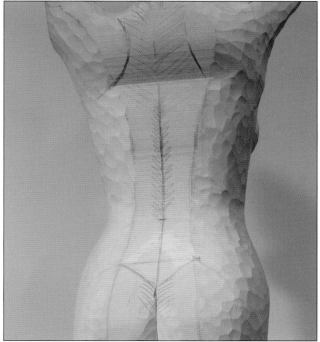

39 Mark the wood to be removed from the spine. At the top of the buttocks this is a deep cleft which quickly flattens out on the sacrum. This is best seen in the photograph on page 17. Just above the sacrum it becomes deep again between the two columns of muscles. Just below the shoulder blade it again starts to flatten out in a shallow depression between the high points of the shoulder blades.

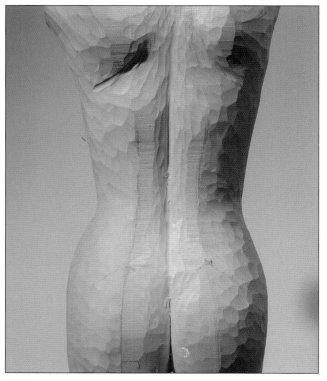

40 Remove the wood from the marked areas.

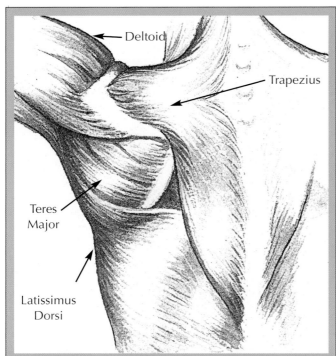

Diagram A: Note that the muscles of the upper back are extremely complex and react strongly to slight movements and stresses on them. They also vary dramatically according to the muscular development of the individual. This subject is only thinly muscled, and just below the neck the vertebrae can be seen protruding.

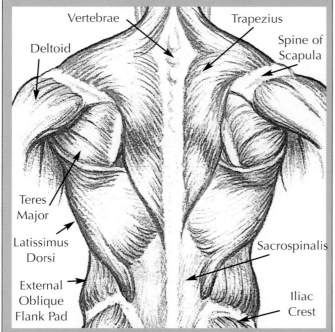

Diagram B: Where the shoulder blade meets the arm, you can see the large bulge of the deltoid muscle and the deep creases where the arm, shoulder blade and collarbone intersect. Notice the hard, straight edge of the trapezius muscle, which attaches to the top edge of the spine of the scapula and runs across the shoulder and up the neck.

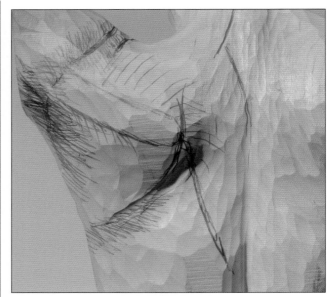

41 The shoulder blades present a difficult area, a mass of bones and muscles in constant movement. Study the photographs on pages 14, 15 and 17 carefully. The light line running diagonally across the shoulder blade (page 17) is the spine of the scapula. The lower end juts out (page 15). The inner edge of the blade curves around from the inner end of the spine toward the outside of the body (page 17) and curves forward (page 17). Mark the waste wood for removal, as shown.

42 Having carved this area, carefully studying the photos along the way, now compare it with the photo on page 17. It is quite good, if a little lumpy.

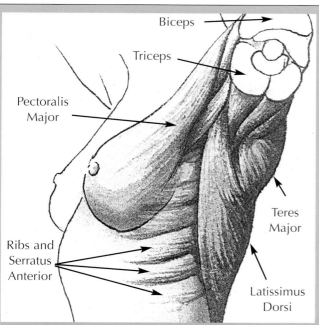

Diagram C: Moving to the front of the shoulder, you find an equally complex arrangement where the pectoral muscle rises up from the chest to engage with the deltoid muscle at the top of the arm. The muscles wrap around the front of the shoulder blade and fold in between the biceps and the triceps. In the triangle between the breast and the shoulder blade, the ribcage, thinly covered, slopes in toward the neck.

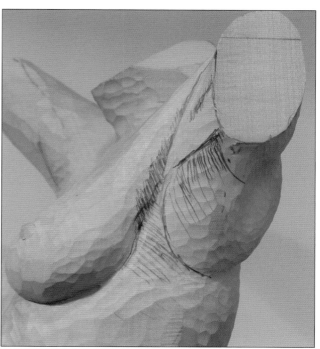

43 Mark the waste wood to be removed along the side of the breast, along the underside of the arm and on the front of the arm, as shown.

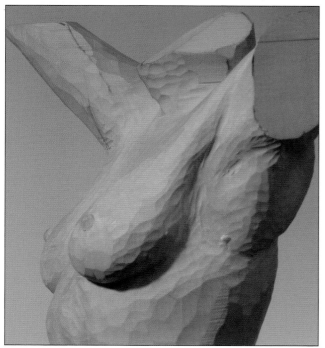

44 The wood has been removed from this area. Note the curved groove formed on the underside of the arm and the slight indentation on the front of the arm.

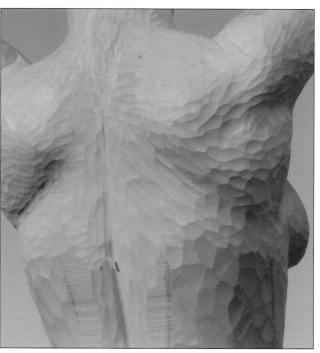

45 The left shoulder is very similar to the right shoulder at the back, but it is slightly further around the body because the arm is angled forward. The high point of the spine of the scapula is less prominent. The deltoid muscle is less swollen and the hollow between the deltoid and the shoulder blade is less pronounced because the arm is not angled upward as much.

46 A view from the front shows the angle of the arm and its effect on the shoulder blade as it moves around toward the front of the body.

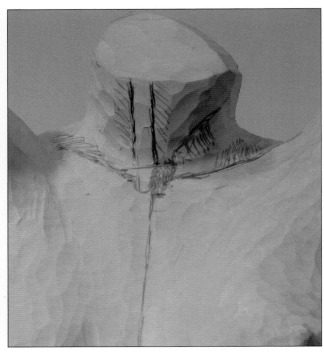

47 Mark the wood to be removed at the neck and collarbones.

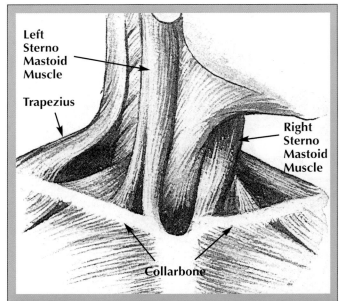

Diagram D: On this model, who has very little body fat and muscle, the left sterno mastoid muscle, running from the back of the ear to the inside end of the left collarbone, is exceptionally prominent. Because of the twist of the head, it runs perfectly in line with the central line of the body. The right sterno mastoid muscle is relaxed and twists from the end of the right collarbone, around the neck and out of sight. Between the two muscles, the windpipe can be seen cutting across at 45 degrees. The collarbones, clearly seen at the front, curve backwards and upwards, disappearing in the muscles of the shoulders.

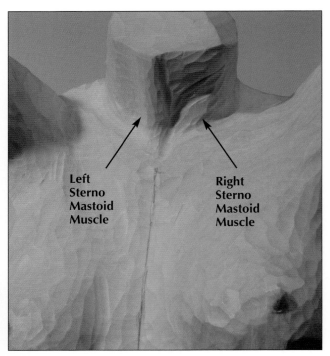

48 This area is now complete. Notice the translation of the left and right sterno mastoid muscles in the wood of the neck.

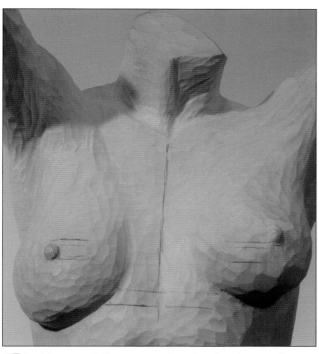

49 After carefully remeasuring the drawings and carvings, it became apparent that the left breast is considerably too low. The lower line on this photo shows the true level. The nipple is only fractionally too low and should be okay.

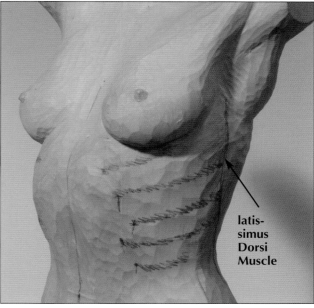

latis-
simus
Dorsi
Muscle

50 The left breast has been raised. On the model the ribs are highly visible, even on the back in some views. If you carve everything as you can see it, the finished torso will look ugly. With this in mind, carve the ribs only as far back as the latissimus dorsi muscle, which runs from the armpit, down around the side to the pelvis at the back. Notice that the fourth rib, marked below the breast, is more prominent than the others.

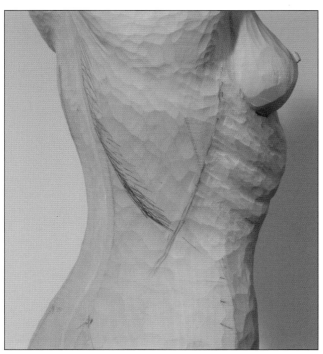

51 Carve in the ribs, and then move to the back. Looking at a photograph of the back (page 17), the shape of the ribcage can be seen as it passes under the column of muscle running up either side of the spine. Mark this area for wood removal.

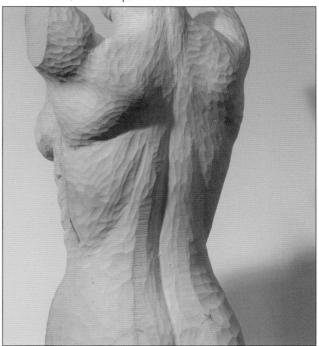

52 The wood has been removed, and the muscles on the spine can now be clearly seen. The line of the ribs runs down and around the side, sharpening the waistline.

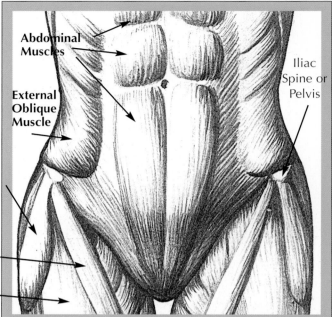

Abdominal Muscles

External Oblique Muscle

Tensor Pasciae Latae

Sartorius

Pectus Femoris

Iliac Spine or Pelvis

Diagram E: Some complicated and quite subtle shapes create the stomach and the hips. On both sides of the centerline are the abdominal muscles. Outside of these are the external oblique muscles that run up and over the ribs. The pelvis is tilted because the bent left leg raises the right corner of the pelvis slightly. The abdominal muscles run down to the pubic bone.

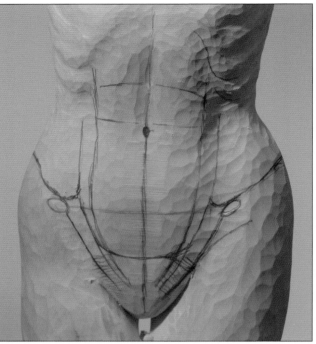

53 Mark the lines of the muscles on the figure. At the bottom of the external oblique, the front corners of the pelvis appear as two small oval lumps. The details can be seen fairly well in the photographs of the model on pages 14, 15 and 16.

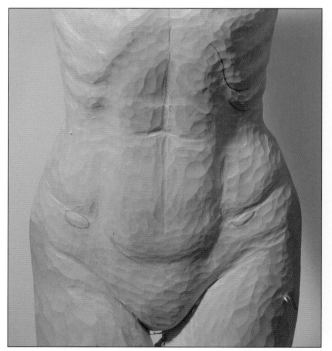

54 The abdominal area has been carved, but it is difficult to finish it completely in isolation from the hips and the thighs.

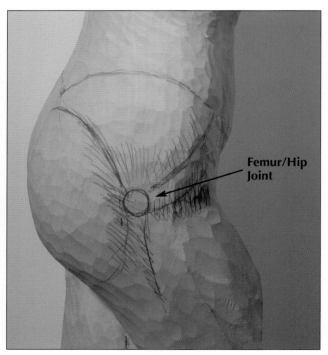

Femur/Hip Joint

55 Mark the muscles on the left hip area. On the left side of the model there is very little definition of the muscle because it is not under tension. This lack of tension creates, more or less, a smooth, curved expanse of flesh. The crease where the leg folds is quite marked, however. The circle is the actual joint at the top of the femur that one can feel and see.

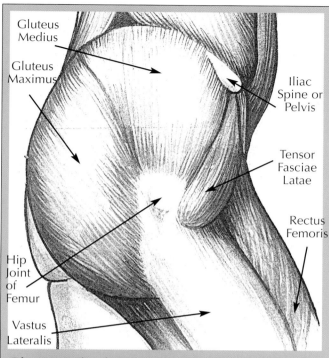

Gluteus Medius

Gluteus Maximus

Iliac Spine or Pelvis

Tensor Fasciae Latae

Rectus Femoris

Hip Joint of Femur

Vastus Lateralis

Diagram F: The gluteus maximus runs off to the back to form the buttock and also upward to attach to the pelvis. At the front another muscle connects from the hip to the front of the pelvis.

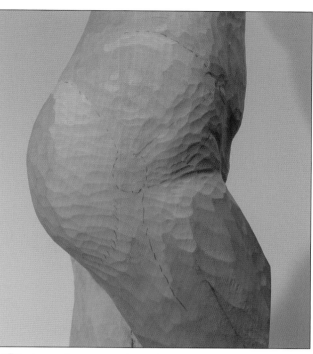

56 Here these areas have been carved.

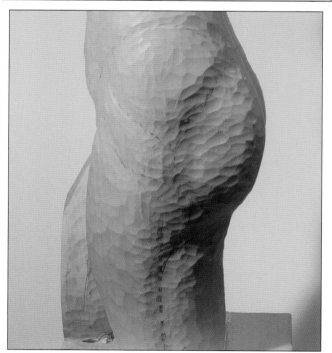

57 The structures on the right side are more clearly defined. The buttock is tightened to support the body, and this causes a deep hollow at the side. This can be seen clearly in the photograph on page 15. On this side there is also a large groove running down the thigh where the big muscles are in tension. Mark and carve these areas now.

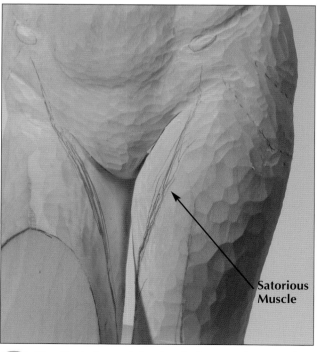

Satorious Muscle

58 The final piece of shaping is the sartorius muscle, which runs from the front of the pelvis and twists around the front of the thigh to the inside back of the knee. Mark these muscles, as shown.

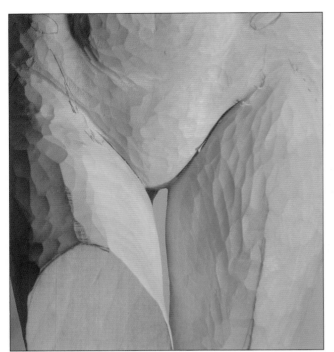

59 The sartonius muscle is a very subtle form. It can be seen in the photograph on page 16 and quite clearly in the photograph on page 14. Although not a strong shape, it does give the characteristic shape to the thigh. Note that the centerlines down the legs still remain.

60 Your carving should now look something like this. If you are a staunch adherent to the tooled finish, you have the difficult task ahead of achieving a surface in keeping with the skin of a young woman. For my own part, I now sand the entire carving with 80-grit sandpaper to achieve a smooth surface.

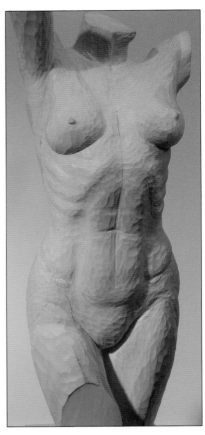

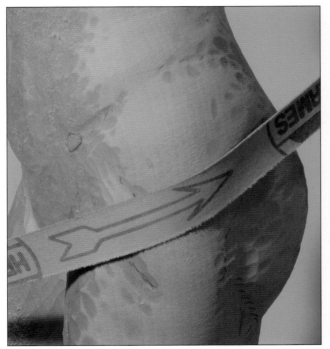

61 Using a strip of quality 80-grit sanding cloth, sand the figure to a uniformly smooth surface. The remains of tool cuts, such as can be seen here, must be totally removed. If they are not eradicated with the coarse grit, they will probably still be there when the polish is put on.

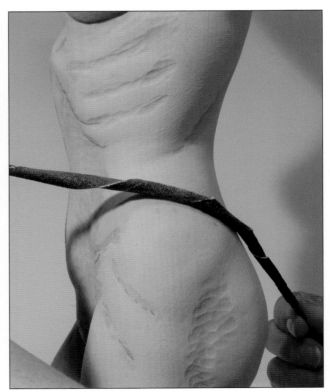

62 Some of the depressions can be sanded by twisting the strip into a tube or by using narrower strips.

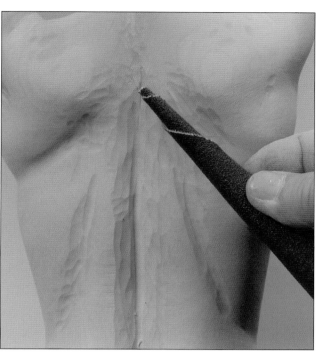

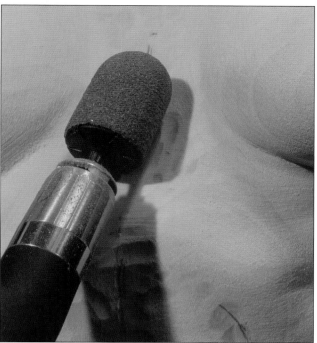

63 Further sanding in more inaccessible spots can be carried out using a square of cloth rolled into a cone. The sanding up to this point has taken exactly one hour. Using good quality materials and the right methods, sanding does not take as long as many people think.

64 In some hollows and grooves, power tools, such as the thumb sander shown here, can be used to remove the tool cuts. Take great care if you use this method, and do not expect these tools to produce a finished surface.

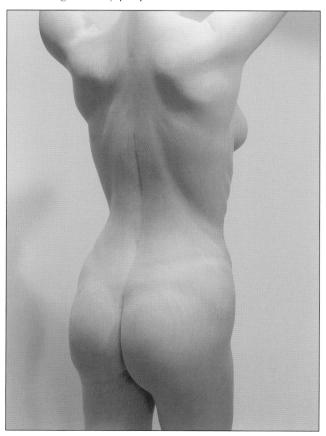

65 The carving is roughly sanded. The problem now is to make it into something desirable. To do that, compare the figure very carefully with the eight photographs of the live model and look for differences. Here's a list of what I found when I compared this photograph of the carving with the photograph of the model on page 17.
• The shoulder blade on the left of the picture is too lumpy.
• The narrow point of the waist on the left side is not at a sharp enough angle. The ribs should slope forward more, and the muscles running from the hips up the spine should be at a tighter angle.
• The profile of the buttock on the left should be flatter. The muscle should be tighter and the buttock narrower.
• The bottom line of the buttock should be higher and flatter.
• The buttock on the right should have a shallower curve.
• The area around the pelvis on the right-hand side should be less rotund and the narrow point of the waist lower and narrower.

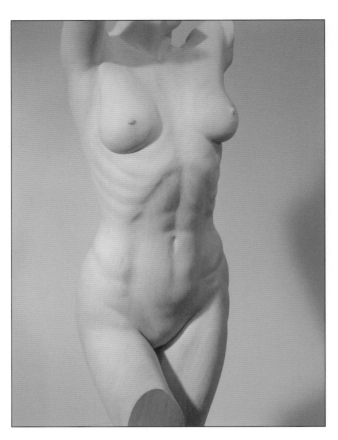

 66 Looking to the front now, compare this photograph of the carving with the photograph of the model on page 15.

• Clearly, the left arm is in a different position to the original pose, but this can be discounted.

• On the right side, the hollow curve of the abdomen should be deeper and smoother. On the model, the curve then drops in quite a smooth line to the leg.

• The curve of the ribs on the left side of the stomach should be smoother.

• The buttock is too bulbous and should move down in a smooth, unbroken curve from waist to the thigh.

• The top of the left thigh on the inside edge should terminate in a shallow curve.

• The central groove above and below the navel needs to be more marked than I have it, and the "bikini line" needs to be clearer.

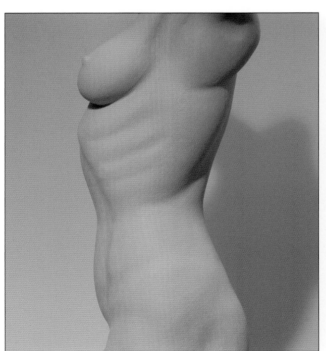

67 I now decided to depart from reality. I felt the ribs needed to be drastically reduced in prominence, so I sanded them down quite brutally. I then put in the navel and the two small depressions in the lower back. (See Step 70.) These depressions can be seen on one or two of the photographs of the model (pages 14 and 17).

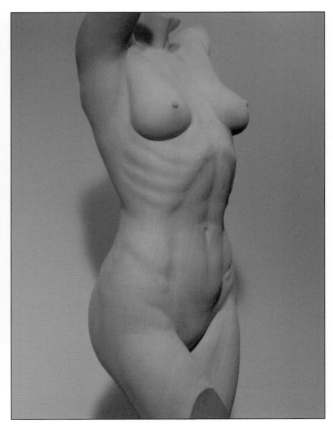

68 The revised carving from another view.

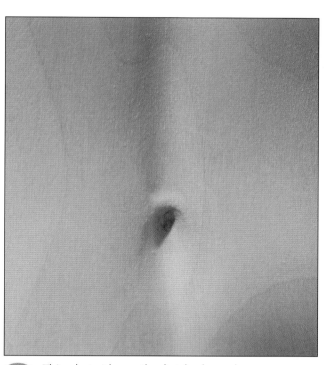

69 This photo shows the finished navel.

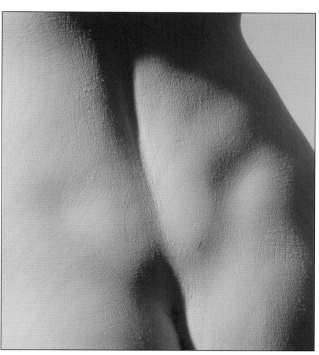

70 Here you can see the modeling on the lower back.

71 Continue sanding up to 240 grit. In sharp corners use folded sandpaper. I have found garnet paper to be best for this purpose because the grit does not flake off when folded. After using the 120-grit paper, wash the carving over boiling water. This raises the grain and brings out any deep scratches, dents or creases. When the carving is completely dry, continue with the sanding.

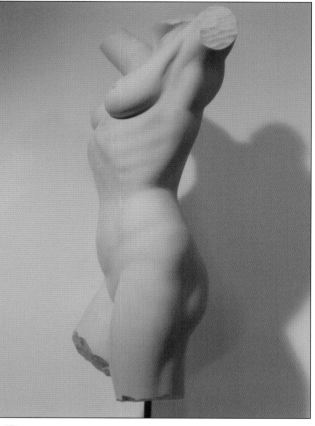

72 When the sanding is completed, cut away the bandsawed ends of the limbs. I prefer a kind of broken look, but a perfectly flat surface square across the limb is quite common in sculpture.

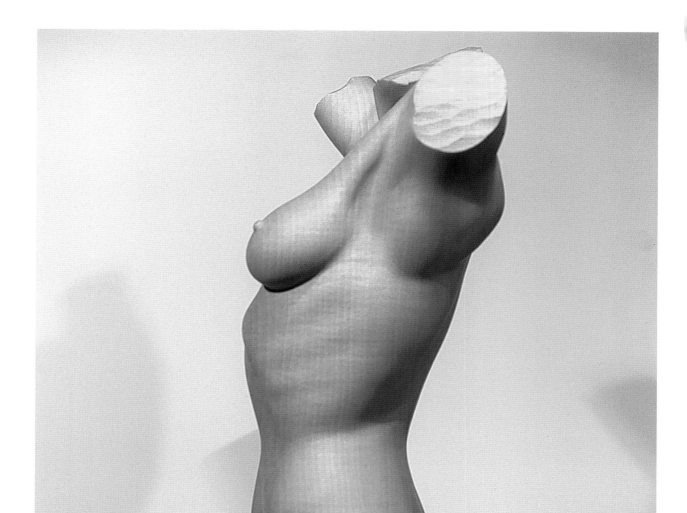

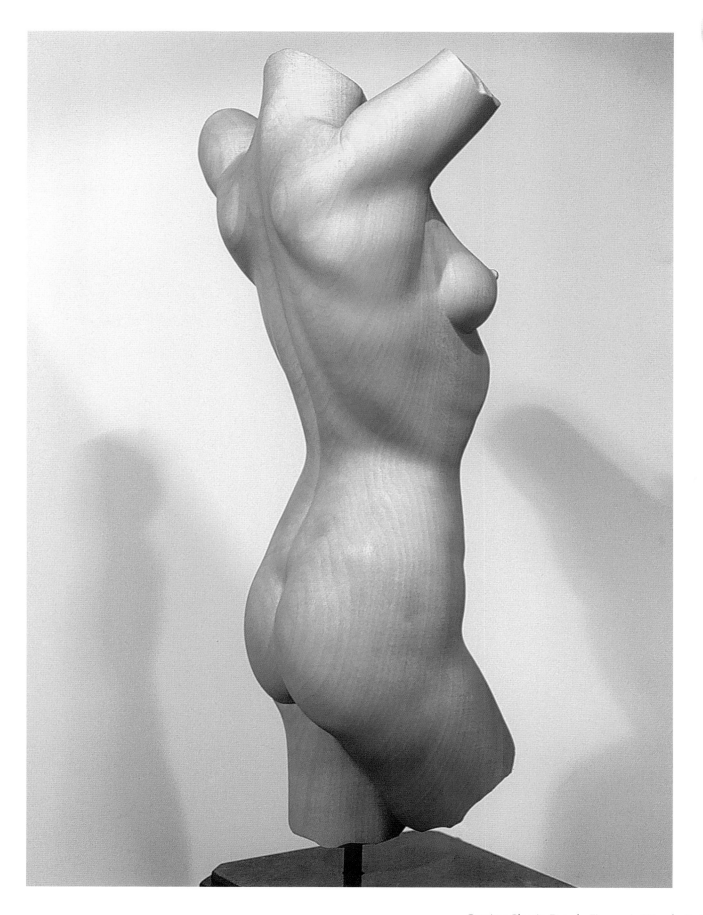

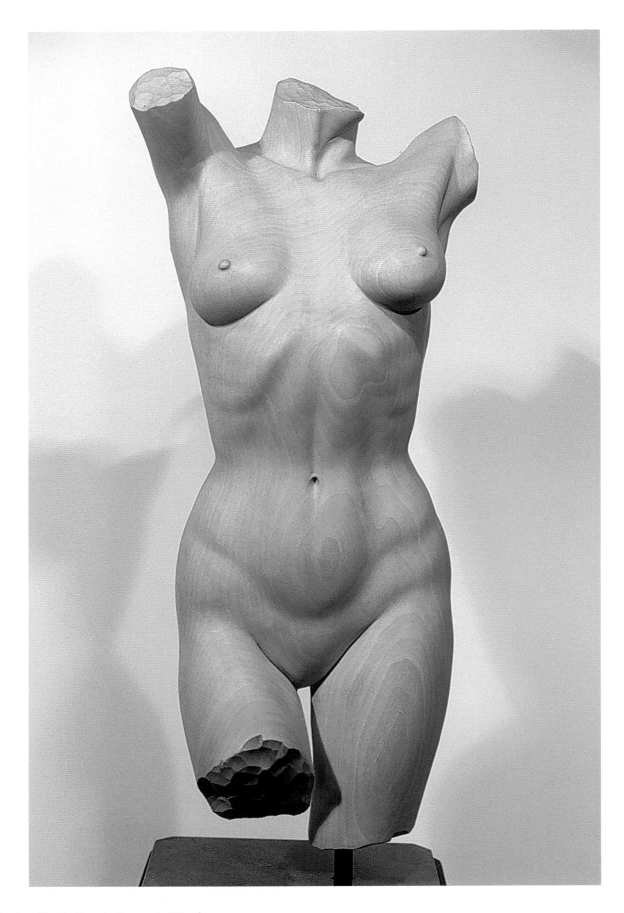

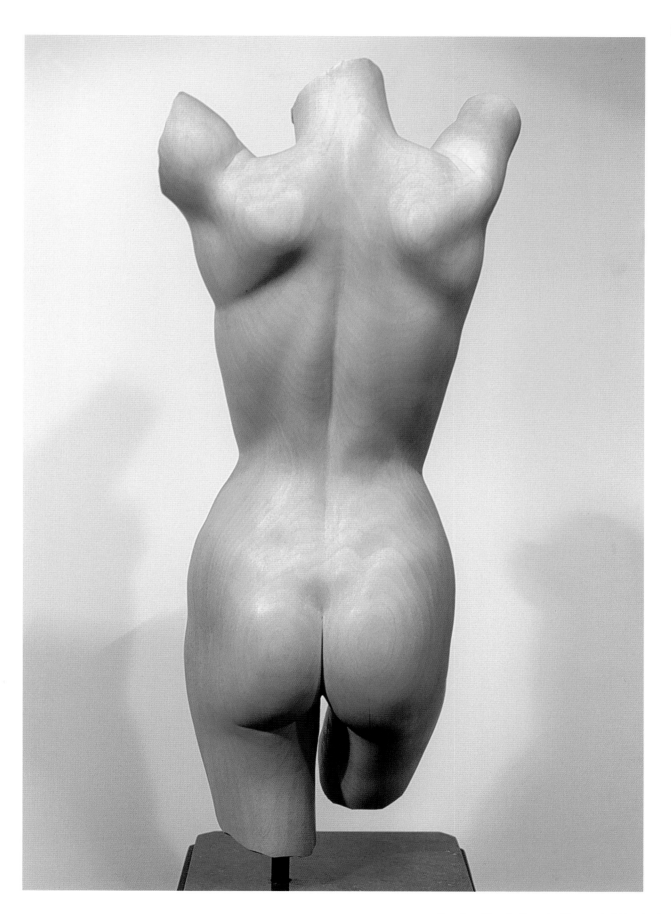

LIMEWOOD TORSO

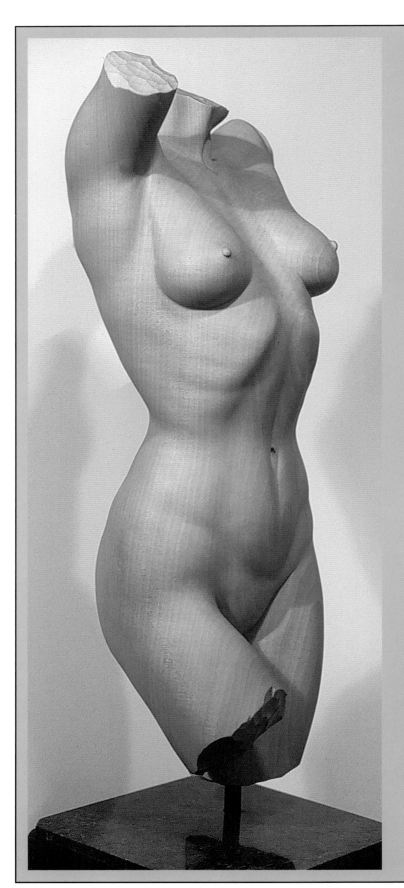

A Perfect Polish

When you are satisfied with the sanded surface (I usually use 80, 120, 180, 240 and 320 grits in progression.), the carving will need some kind of finish to enhance the wood and to protect it. Wood finishing is a huge subject, and theories and methods abound. Basically, you have two choices: Either employ a professional to do it for you or use a simple method yourself.

For years I used sanding sealer, followed by a wax polish. On simpler shapes, such as this torso, this kind of finish looks and feels very good. However, it is difficult to apply a wax finish on complex and fragile carvings; fine details can get clogged with wax. A wax finish also needs maintenance, which means that the person who owns the carving has to wax it now and then. Some people overdo it, and the piece ends up very shiny. Others neglect it, and the piece ends up dull and dusty. The fragile pieces often get broken.

The method I now use is to brush on a polyurethane varnish, not too sticky, and then immediately wipe it off with kitchen towels–and I mean really wipe it, as if you were getting a dirty mark off of the wood. In corners, wipe the varnish off with a dry brush. This leaves a very thin layer, with no brush marks, runs or puddles, that dries so quickly it does not get dusty. When the varnish is dry, repeat the process three or four times. I use a matte varnish, which gives a satiny finish, is waterproof and durable and never needs to be touched again.

CARVING A
WALNUT TORSO

The first project in this book was a very straightforward pose designed to give you an easy introduction to the female form. This second project is a far more energetic pose. To carve this piece requires good photographs, good working drawings and an ability to grasp three-dimensional shapes. The third item is something you will learn as you carve this and other female figures.

I decided to use walnut for this figure because its beautiful color and grain will add to the movement and vibrancy of the finished piece. Also this torso is very small, and I find it very pleasing o use the more valuable and exotic woods, which are usually only available in small dimensions on these small scale projects. The timber itself gives the piece a quality that would not be present if limewood were used.

10″ high

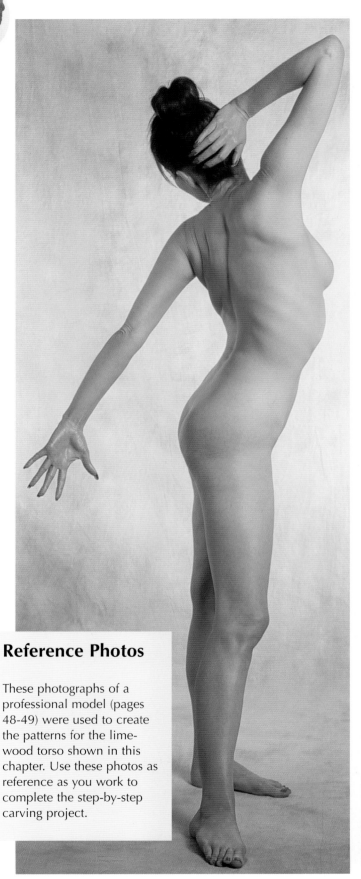

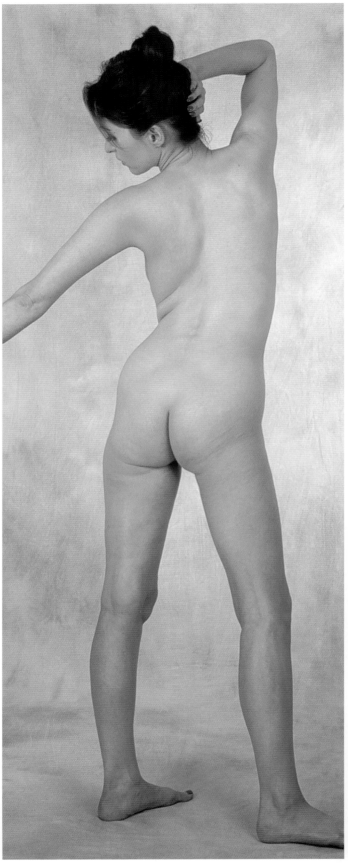

Reference Photos

These photographs of a professional model (pages 48-49) were used to create the patterns for the lime-wood torso shown in this chapter. Use these photos as reference as you work to complete the step-by-step carving project.

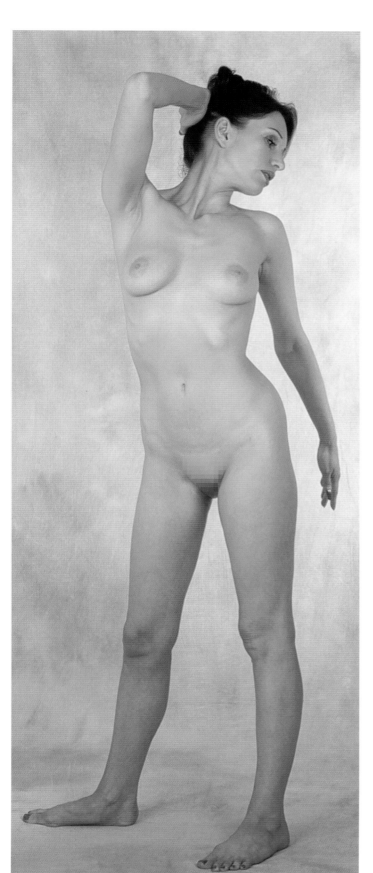

Walnut Torso
©Ian Norbury

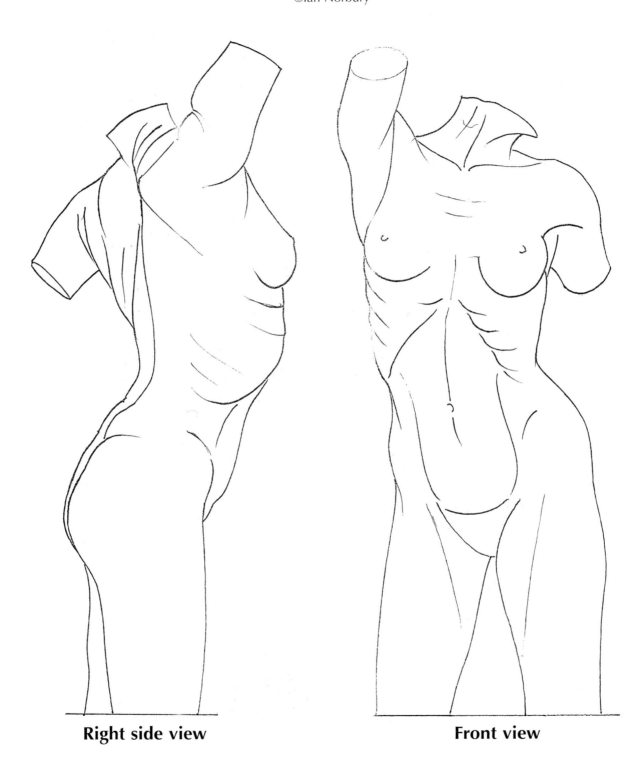

Right side view   **Front view**

Use the front and side views shown here to bandsaw the blank. Cut very carefully, precisely on the line. Remember that tracing the plans onto a block of wood and bandsawing them allows for considerable accumulative errors. Only by taking great care can you reduce these errors to a minimum.

Walnut Torso
©Ian Norbury

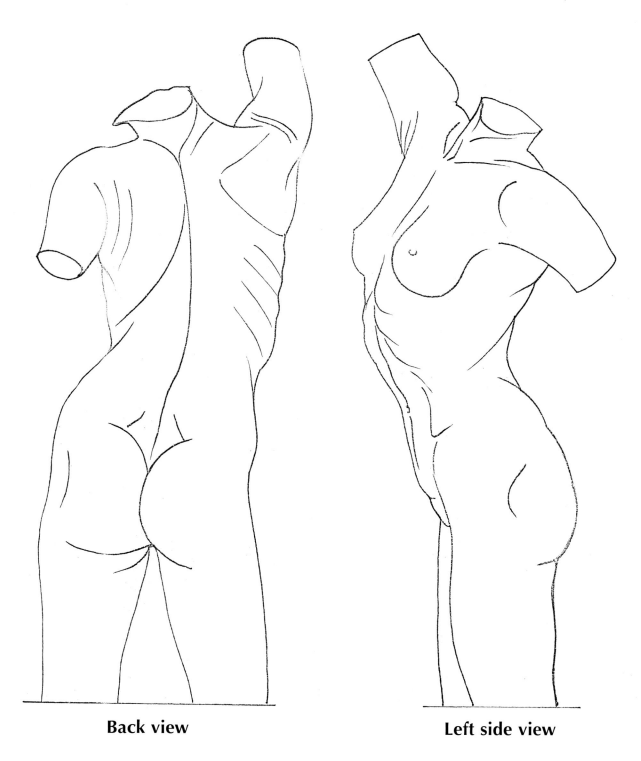

Back view

Left side view

The back and opposite side views are provided to show carving details.

WALNUT TORSO

1 All the preparatory work is done in exactly the same way as the first project. Here the bandsawed block (11″ x 4″ x 4″) is ready to have the waste removed in front of the right shoulder. Cut this as a curved corner, not as a square cut. (See Step 6.)

2 Cut away the waste wood extending from the right arm across the back and the small block in line with the neck.

3 Remove the waste wood at the back. Note the curve where it meets the arm. This is not a square corner. Mark the line of the spine on the back and on the side. This area can be cut away to a square corner.

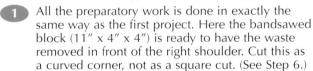

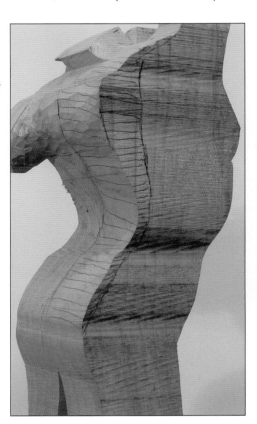

4 The right-hand side of the back has been reduced. The corner remaining between the arm and the back can now be carved in a curve where the shoulder is pulled back.

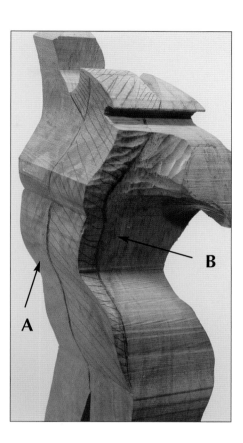

6 Draw the centerline on the front (A). On the right side draw the line running from the front of the neck, down the right side of the chest and ribs, and down to the bottom of the stomach (B). Cut this area into a corner. The block of waste in front of the neck can be cut away across to the left shoulder.

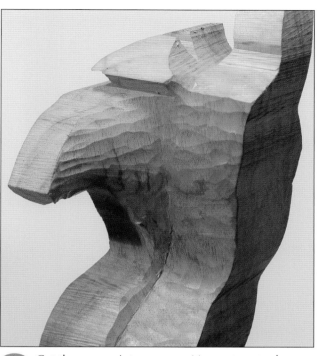

5 Cut the corner into a curve. Now return to the front of the figure.

7 Cut back the right side of the front. These processes may seem strange and drastic, but it is the best way to achieve a positive twist to the body. Measure and cut to size the front of the right leg and the rear of the left leg.

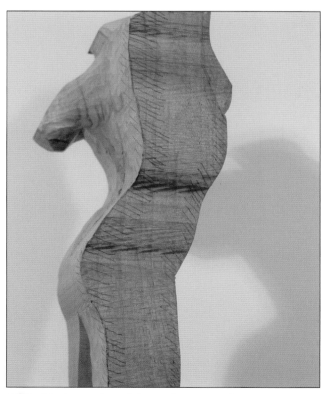

8 Having reduced the major areas of waste, you can now round off the corners. I did most of this with a round Surform rasp.

9 Shape the corner between the left arm and the neck into a curve where the muscle is pulled upward. Slope the right shoulder where it is pulled back by the arm.

10 Round the right arm and shoulder.

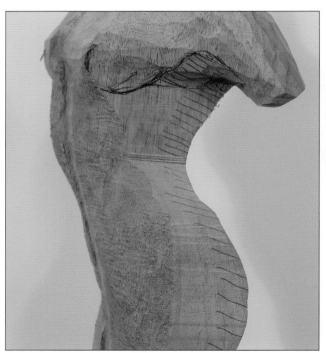

11 Locate the side view of the right breast and armpit. Cut into the armpit, and then round off the corner of the body.

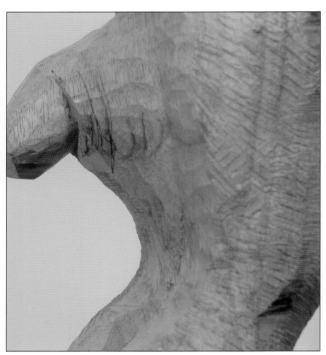

12 Moving to the back, cut in the deep folds behind the right shoulder and establish the dimension of the upper arm.

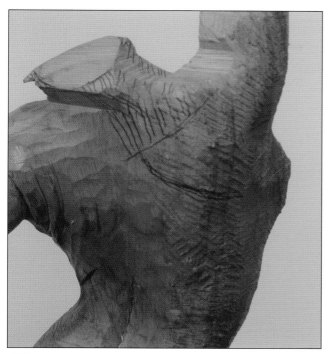

13 Round the neck and blend it into the back of the left shoulder.

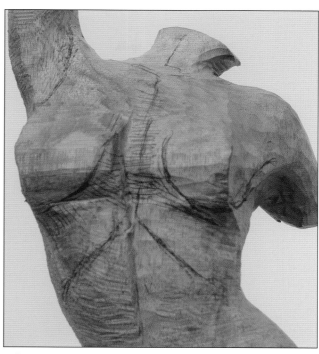

14 Mark the approximate lines of the breasts and the ribs. Cut away the waste between the breasts and round them off. Lightly cut in the lines of the ribs.

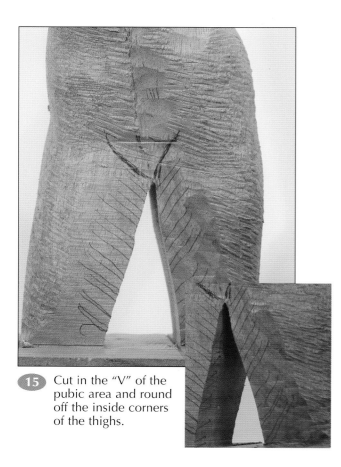

15 Cut in the "V" of the pubic area and round off the inside corners of the thighs.

16 Cut in the division of the buttocks and round off the inside rear corners of the thighs.

17 The basic form of the figure should now be roughly established. Clean up the surface using files.

18 Using the anatomical diagrams and relating them to the photographs of the model, draw the main features onto the figure.

19 Cut these features in with gouges. By using this diagrammatic method, you have a positive system for establishing the physical features, even though they may not correspond to the particular model.

20 Repeat the same process on the back.

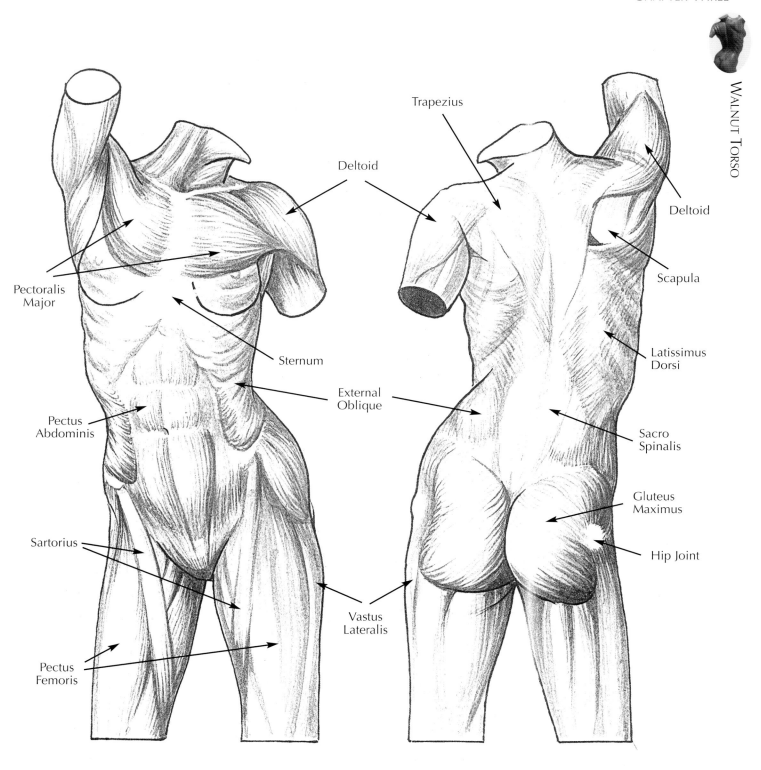

Trapezius

Deltoid

Deltoid

Scapula

Pectoralis
Major

Sternum

Latissimus
Dorsi

Pectus
Abdominis

External
Oblique

Sacro
Spinalis

Gluteus
Maximus

Sartorius

Hip Joint

Pectus
Femoris

Vastus
Lateralis

Diagram H: These anatomical sketches show the major muscle groups that come into play on a carving in this pose. Use these drawings in combination with the photographs to identify the cuts that will define this carving.

21 Rough sand the entire figure with 80-grit sandpaper.

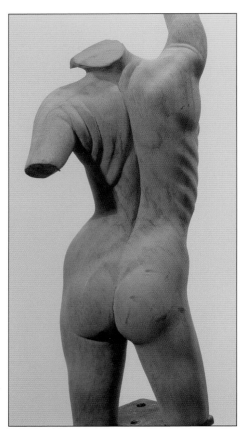

22 The back of the figure is rough sanded as well. In your final review of the project, look for discrepancies in the shapes of the ribs and pelvis, which are rigid and do not alter, regardless of movement.

Views of the finished piece from above and below show the dynamic twists in this torso. It is important to look down from the top of the figure, as well as across from the side, as you carve to ensure that the twist of the body is not resulting in deformities.

WALNUT TORSO

WALNUT TORSO

More Great Project Books from Fox Chapel Publishing

Carving Classic Female Faces in Wood
By Ian Norbury
Learn to sculpt the female face in wood from renowned woodcarver and instructor, Ian Norbury. The author not only teaches the fundamentals of woodcarving, but also demonstrates how to accurately and realistically portray the female face in wood. Clear, step-by-step photographs with instructional captions guide you though an entire carving project. This is a must-have reference for anyone interested in getting started or improving their realistic facial carving.
ISBN: 1-56523-102-3, 88 pages, soft cover, $17.95

Art of Ian Norbury: Sculptures in Wood
By Ian Norbury
This gallery of carvings features the work of Ian Norbury, one of the world's leading sculptors, whose innovative style incorporates materials including mixed timber, colored wood, metals, stones, shells, and gems. Photographs richly illustrate his art, inspired by masters such as Salvador Dali, René Magritte, and Mexican surrealist Remedios Varro.
ISBN: 1-56523-222-4, 128 pages, soft cover, $24.95

Carving the Female Face
By Wally Lueth
Carving the female face in wood presents a difficult challenge for woodcarvers. Starting with photos of women's faces, this guide offers an anatomy lesson on the bone and muscle structure of the female face, including information on the facial features of women. Detailed instructions on how these delicate features can be convincingly carved are presented through sixteen ready-to-use patterns.
ISBN: 1-56523-145-7, 72 pages, soft cover, $12.95

Caricature Carving from Head to Toe
By Dave Stetson
Find out what makes a carving "caricature" with this top-notch guide from Dave Stetson. First you will learn how anatomy relates to expression by creating a clay mold. Then, you will follow the author step-by-step through an entire carving project for an Old Man with Walking Stick. Additional patterns for alternate facial expressions, overview of wood selection, tools, and an expansive photo gallery also included.
ISBN: 1-56523-121-X, 96 pages, soft cover, $19.95

Carving Eyes
By Jeff Phares
Life-like, expressive eyes are the key to successful human carvings and now you can learn how to create them with world-renowned carver, Jeff Phares. Learn to carve an average eye, a heavy-lidded eye, a baggy eye, a winking eye, and a sleeping eye. Includes over 200 step-by-step photos.
ISBN: 1-56523- 163-5, 72 pages, soft cover, $14.95.

Carving Ears and Hair
By Jeff Phares
Learn the art of carving authentic looking ears and hair with world-renowned carver, Jeff Phares. Learn the secrets to carving realistic ears through photographs from several angles, drawings, and step-by-step instructions. Then, learn to carve curly and braided hair in a similar teaching style.
ISBN: 1-56523-164-3, 72 pages, soft cover, $14.95.

Carving the Nose & Mouth
By Jeff Phares
Carve perfect noses and mouths with help from world-renowned carver, Jeff Phares. This book includes extensive step-by-step demonstrations, close-up photos and anatomy information on Native American and Caucasian faces.
ISBN: 1-56523-161-9, 72 pages, soft cover, $14.95.

Art of Stylized Wood Carving
By Charles Solomon and Dave Hamilton
Learn to capture beauty and expression in wood with the art of stylized carving. This book features interviews, artwork from top carvers, and 5 step-by-step carving demonstrations for canvasback duck, hummingbird, bottlenose dolphin, shelf-sitting mouse, and rainbow trout.
ISBN: 1-56523-174-0, 112 pages, soft cover, $19.95.

Inspirational Relief Carving
By William Judt
Learn to express your faith in wood with over 20 relief carving projects inspired by Scripture. First, you will learn the basics of relief carving. Then, you will follow the author, step-by-step as he demonstrates how to carve a house blessing featuring a cross with a descending dove. Not to be missed is a section on marketing your carvings.
ISBN: 1-56523-205-4, 112 pages, soft cover, $19.95.

CHECK WITH YOUR LOCAL BOOK OR WOODWORKING STORE
Or call 800-457-9112 • Visit www.FoxChapelPublishing.com